MW00760301

This Book is dedicated to

Rosie O'Donnell

for all the love, care, and help she delivers to children
through her foundation "For All Kids."

Printed in China.
Graphic Art by Dr. Hope.

Library of Congress Catalog Number: 99-63177

PUNCTUATION PALS/by Dr. Hope, J.A.P.D.

Summary: Mr. Period teaches how to use proper punctuation.
1. Punctuation—Fiction 2.Punctuation—Text. I. Title.

99-63177
ISBN 1-885624-56-5

FIRST EDITION

Punctuation Pals

Written by Dr. Hope, J.A.P.D.

(Just **A** **P**retend **D**octor)

Illustrated by Richard Pinson

Hi there! I'm Mr. Period, the little guy who is going to introduce you to some important new friends.

To show you how important they are, here is a little story I think you will enjoy. I'm proud to say I was chosen for the starring role. I hope you like it; here it is!

One day Mr. Period was walking down a paragraph looking for the end of a sentence when all of a sudden he stubbed his toe on a misspelled word .

"Ouch!" he yelped.

"What happened**?**" asked the curious Ms. Question Mark .

"I don't know**!**" said an extremely upset Ms. Colon, "Someone

might have tried to use Mr. Period in the middle of a sentence, or

maybe something even worse, like *bad grammar!*"

"Gasp! Not *bad grammar!*" blurted out Mr. Exclamation Point.

All the Punctuation Pals shuddered like this : tremble, quiver, shiver .

They all hoped it wasn't anything *that* frightful.

"We were there marking his word, 'Ouch!' right after it happened," replied Mr. Open Quotation Mark and Mr. Close Quotation Mark, "but we don't know exactly what occurred either."

"He looks like he may have hurt himself," said Mr. and Mrs. Parentheses. (They were very concerned too.)

"I saw the whole thing; he just stubbed his toe on a misspelled word. If we correct the word, I'm sure he will be just fine," said Mr. Comma as he busily corrected the word.

"Mr. Period, are you all right?" asked Ms. Question Mark.
"I'm fine now that Mr. Comma corrected the misspelled word,"
said Mr. Period. "Thank you all so much for your help and concern."

I was pretty good, wasn't I? Please hold your applause down to a loud roar; you wouldn't want me to get a fat head would you? (Wink.) Okay, let's get down to business. Do you know what made that story easy to read? That's right! It was my Punctuation Pals. I'm going to explain how to use us whenever you write.

First, I—Mr. Period—am the traffic cop for all written words. A mighty big job for just a small dot, but without me you'd never know where to stop before another thought started. I let you know when the statement is done. That's my main job. So when you see me, stop—then go on to the next sentence.

This is my pal, Mr. Comma. He is my assistant traffic officer. When you see him you don't have to stop like when you see me, you just slow down and pause a little bit. His job is to make you pause between separate thoughts within a sentence.

This is my good friend, Mr. Exclamation Point, but watch your ears, he's always excited and yelling his sentences.
Mr. Exclamation Point, please say hello to our readers.

"HELLO! GOSH! SOMEONE IS READING THIS BOOK! GREAT! I'M SO EXCITED!" cried out Mr. Exclamation Point.

We use Mr. Exclamation Point to show when a thought is said loudly or with excitement. (Like this: HELP!) Mr. Exclamation Point lives at the end of sentences just like I do.

This is Ms. Question Mark. You put her at the end of a sentence when a question is being asked. Say something to the nice readers, Ms. Question Mark.

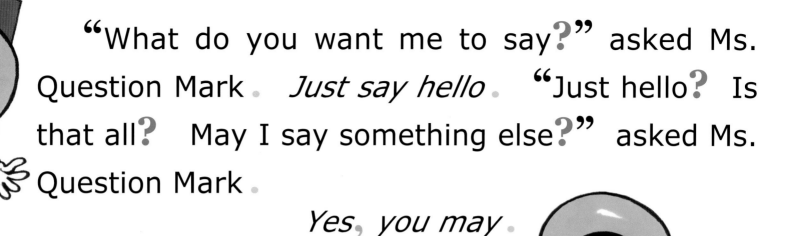

"What do you want me to say?" asked Ms. Question Mark. *Just say hello.* "Just hello? Is that all? May I say something else?" asked Ms. Question Mark.

Yes, you may.

"Did you know my mind is so full of questions I can't think of anything to say?

I know, have you met my girlfriends, Ms. Colon and Ms. Semicolon?" asked Ms. Question Mark.

I was just going to introduce them.

This is Ms. Colon . You use her like this : to give an example, to make an explanation, or to list a series .

And this is my cousin Ms. Semicolon. When you see her, you almost make a complete stop, but not quite. She separates thoughts that are closely related. She's very useful; that's a fact.

Now it's time for you to meet my beloved friends, Mr. and Mrs. Parentheses. They're such a loving couple, you never see one without the other following close behind.

Their job is to separate an added remark (like whispering to you in the middle of a conversation) from the main direction of the thought .   See how easy that was?

These are the twins, Mr. Open Quotation Mark and Mr. Close Quotation Mark. They surround exact words that someone has said. Please say hello to the nice readers.

"Hi, I'm Mr. Open Quotation Mark; I'm always first. I let you know when someone has started saying something," said Mr. Open Quotation Mark.

"Hello, I'm Mr. Close Quotation Mark; I'm always last. I let you know when someone is finished saying something," said Mr. Close Quotation Mark.

Okay, now that you know all of my punctuation pals, it's time for some fun stuff. You get to use all your new pals to punctuate the following story. I think you might recognize it. Ready? Here we go!

Without proper punctuation everything can get all jumbled together. Can you fix the story on the next page by putting the Punctuation Pals where they belong?

Your Punctuation Pals are on the last page of this book, just waiting to be peeled and stuck onto the right spot.

(Hint: All the Punctuation Pals are color coded.)

One day Mr. Period was walking down a paragraph looking for the end of a sentence when all of a sudden he stubbed his toe on a misspelled word_

Ouch _ he yelped_

What happened _ asked the curious Ms. Question Mark_

I don't know _ said an extremely upset Ms. Colon_ _Someone might have tried to use Mr. Period in the middle of a sentence_ or maybe something even worse_ like *bad grammar_* _

Gasp Not *bad grammar_* _ blurted out Mr. Exclamation Point_ All the Punctuation Pals shuddered like this_ tremble_quiver_ shiver_ They all hoped it wasn't anything *that* frightful_

We were there marking his word 'Ouch_' right after it happened_ _ replied Mr. Open Quotation Mark and Mr. Close Quotation Mark_ _but we don't know exactly what occurred either_ _

He looks like he may have hurt himself _ said Mr. and Mrs. Parentheses_ _They were very concerned too_ _

I saw the whole thing he just stubbed his toe on a misspelled word_ If we correct the word_ I'm sure he will be just fine_ _ said Mr. Comma as he busily corrected the word_

Mr. Period are you all right _ _ asked Ms. Question Mark_

I'm fine now that Mr. Comma corrected the misspelled word _ said Mr. Period_ _Thank you all so much for your help and concern_ _

Thanks for putting my Punctuation Pals back in their homes.

(You can check your answers against the story in the beginning of the book.)

Remember to use us the next time you write .

Thanks and happy writing .   ' Bye .

Author Dr. Hope wants you to know about

ChildhelpUSA

a non-profit organization that tirelessly fights child abuse.
You can help too.
If you suspect that a child is being neglected or abused,
please call the child abuse hot line at:

1 800 4 A CHILD

They can help. On behalf of that child we thank you.

Storybooks, Cassettes and CD's by Dr. Hope, J.A.P.D.

24 hour toll free order line: **(800) 549 7080**

Laughing Day

A young elf learns a valuable lesson and teaches it to others. A marvelous transformation occurs during the Laughing Day Celebration.

The Frog Who Couldn't Jump

Freddie the Frog learns that you don't have to come in first to be a winner.

Chip, the Little Computer (written in English and Spanish)

Chip, the Little Computer learns the power of determination and believing in your dream.

The Laughing Day Cassette

The Laughing Day story is acted out by talented voice actors along with five humorous original songs written and performed by Russ T. Nailz.

Chip, the Little Computer CD

Chip, the Little Computer story is acted out by talented voice actors along with five humorous original songs written and performed by Russ T. Nailz.

The Frog Who Couldn't Jump CD

The Frog Who Couldn't Jump story is acted out by talented voice actors along with five humorous original songs written and performed by Russ T. Nailz.

Also available are: Punctuation Pals, The Frog Who Couldn't Jump, Chip, the Little Computer and Laughing Day coloring books.

Visit Dr. Hope's **FREE** Game & Music Website at:

www.laughingday.com

I'm Mr. Period, stop when you see me at the end of a sentence .

. . . .

I'm Mr. Comma, slow down when you see me .

, , , , , , , , , , , , ,

I'm Mr. Exclamation Point, use me to show excitement .

! ! ! ! !

I'm Ms. Question Mark, I show you when a question is being asked .

? ?

I'm Ms. Colon, use me before an example, an explanation, or a series .

:

I'm Ms. Semicolon, use me to seperate closely related thoughts within a sentence .

;

We're Mr. & Mrs. Parentheses, use us to quietly whisper a thought .

( )

We're the Quotation Marks, use us before and after someone says something .

" "